# FOSSIL FIND

## By Rose Howell
## Illustrated by David Opie

CELEBRATION PRESS
Pearson Learning Group

# Contents

# Chapter 1

# Dinosaur Time

"My tail fell off!" said Kam.

"I guess that means no more wagging for you!" Eddie said, laughing.

"We can fix it," Luis said. Using wet paper mixed with glue, he helped Kam fix her papier-mâché dinosaur.

Mrs. Day said, "I have news for you, class. I told a reporter from the newspaper about the dinosaurs you are making for the school science fair. Yesterday after school, she came to our classroom and saw your dinosaurs. Now the people at the newspaper have agreed to help us take a dinosaur trip."

"What's a dinosaur trip?" asked Eddie.

"We are going to a dinosaur dig," said Mrs. Day. "A group of scientists and college students are working on a dinosaur dig at Big Bend National Park. We're going to camp there for a weekend and help them find dinosaur fossils. The newspaper will pay for most of our trip, but we need to raise money to pay for food. We'll need tents, too. Let's write a letter to the owner of the sporting goods store to see if we can borrow some tents."

"Sleeping in tents will be a lot of fun," said Tasha.

"Going to a real dig site will be cool!" exclaimed Luis.

"I'm pretty excited myself," said Mrs. Day. "I've prepared a note for you to take home. It explains the trip and asks for volunteer parents to come along."

123 Highland Rd.
Hometown, TX 77777
October 1

Mr. George Spinoza
Spinoza Sporting Goods
456 Main St.
Hometown, TX  77777

Dear Mr. Spinoza,
   We are students in Mrs. Day's class at
Rider Elementary School. We love
dinosaurs. We are going to a real dinosaur
dig at Big Bend National Park. We need to
camp out there. Could you please lend us
some tents? A newspaper reporter is
going to write an article about the dig,
and your store will be mentioned in her
article. Thank you very much.

                    Sincerely,

                    Mrs. Day's students

# Dino Dollars

Mr. Spinoza, the owner of the sporting goods store, called the school. He told Mrs. Day he would be happy to lend tents to the class.

Mrs. Day told the class the good news. "How will we raise money for the food we'll bring on the trip?" she asked.

"We could make dinosaur cookies and sell them at school," said Luis. "My mom has dinosaur cookie cutters."

"We can make chocolate chip *Triceratops* cookies!" said Eddie. "Yum!"

Kam suggested selling lemonade at the science fair. "We could give away a dinosaur fact with every glass that we sell," she said.

"Those are good ideas," Mrs. Day said.

The class decided that they would take turns standing by the dinosaur display at the science fair and selling cookies and lemonade.

For days they drew and cut out paper dinosaurs. The students wrote one dinosaur fact on each paper dinosaur.

On the night of the science fair, the students sold gallons of lemonade. People bought one glass after another.

"I think we've made a lot of money tonight for the trip," said Kam. "Science fairs must make people thirsty."

"Maybe they shouldn't have looked at the desert display!" said Eddie.

At another table Mrs. Day's students sold the cookies that some parents had baked. Trays were filled with chocolate chip dinosaur cookies.

"These cookies are selling fast," said Tasha.

"Dinosaur dig, here we come!" exclaimed Luis.

Kam came over to the cookie table. "How are cookie sales going?" she asked. Just then someone bumped into her. She fell against the table and knocked a tray of cookies to the floor.

"First my dinosaur lost its tail, and now these cookies are crumbs," she said. "I'm just not lucky with dinosaurs!"

# Ready, Set, Go

A few weeks after the science fair, the class was ready to go camping for the weekend. It was Friday afternoon, and school had just let out. A bus was parked in front of the school. Parents and students crowded around the bus.

A truck from the sporting goods store was also parked there. Some of the parents were unloading tents from the truck.

"Did you ever sleep in a tent before?" Kam asked Tasha.

"No, but I can hardly wait," said Tasha. "It will be fun!"

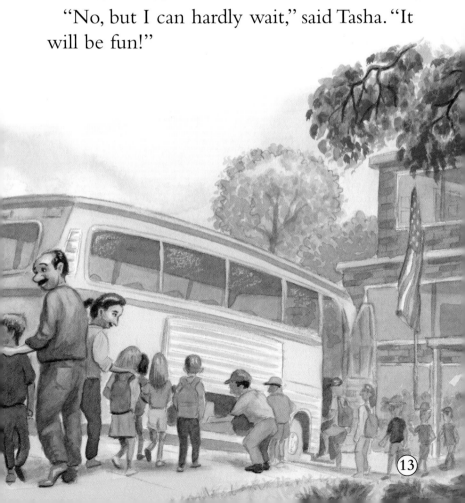

Mrs. Day stood next to the bus with a clipboard. She checked off boxes next to the names of each student to be sure they had hats and water bottles. Then she collected the permission slips.

"I can't find my permission slip," said Luis. He started emptying his backpack. It was a bit messy.

"I'll help you find it," said Kam.

"I hope you're good at finding things," said Eddie. "Luis needs his slip to come on the dinosaur dig!"

*Maybe my luck will change and I'll find the slip for Luis,* thought Kam.

"Here it is!" said Luis.

*I couldn't even find the permission slip,* thought Kam. *How will I find dinosaur fossils?*

"We're ready to go," said Mrs. Day. "Let's get on the bus."

# Dinosaur Dig

It was nearly dark when the bus entered the park. Mrs. Day stopped at a visitors' center while the children stayed on the bus. At last the bus drove to a campsite. After a brown bag dinner, the students and parents set up the tents.

"I love camping!" Tasha whispered to Kam. It was hard for the students to fall asleep that night.

The next morning, Mrs. Day paired each student with a buddy. "We all have hats, walking shoes, and water bottles," she said. "We're ready to help with the dinosaur dig."

At the dig site, the class met the experts who were working on the dig. The first person they met was Dr. Brown.

"I'm a university professor, and I'm also the head paleontologist on this dig," he explained. "Does anyone know what a paleontologist does?"

"A paleontologist is the kind of scientist who studies ancient animals and plants," Luis answered.

"That's right," said Dr. Brown. "Your class can help us do just that."

Mrs. Day's students helped by measuring and pulling string to mark off small dig areas. Next, they began digging. They helped put soil from each area into a bucket. Then the college students carried the buckets to a large screen that sifted the soil. Every now and then, they found tiny fossils.

"Use this paintbrush to gently brush away the dirt from that fossil," said a scientist to Tasha and Kam, pointing.

"You do it," Kam told her friend. "With my luck, I might break it!"

As Tasha bent over, her hat fell off. A small gust of wind blew it.

"I'll get it," said Kam.

Kam ran after Tasha's hat. The wind kept blowing it farther away. Her foot smashed into something, and she fell.

"Ouch!" yelled Kam, rubbing her ankle. She looked around to see what had made her fall. She saw something white sticking up out of the ground.

"I found something!" she called.

# Lost and Found

Everyone ran to see what Kam had found. They found her on the ground.

"Did you hurt yourself?" Mrs. Day asked, sounding worried.

"My ankle hurts a little," Kam said. "Look! That's what made me trip!"

One of the parents brought a first-aid kit. While Mrs. Day checked on Kam's ankle, Dr. Brown looked at the thing that had made Kam trip. It was part of a white bone sticking out of the ground.

"I think you've found a fossil, Kam!" exclaimed Dr. Brown. "We'll take a look and see what it is."

Mrs. Day wrapped tape around Kam's ankle. Then two college students helped Kam back to her tent.

Later that afternoon, Kam limped out of her tent. Dr. Brown had come to speak to her.

"Maybe the bone is from a brand-new dinosaur, Kam," said Eddie. "They could call it a Kam-ankle-asaurus."

"Actually, we think we know what kind of bone it is," said Dr. Brown. "It's from an *Alamosaurus*, one of the last dinosaurs that ever lived and one of the biggest. Several of these dinosaurs have been found here at Big Bend. We think Kam has found another one. The bone that tripped Kam seems to be one of the neck bones."

"Wow!" Eddie said.

"Dr. Brown, what happens to the bone next?" Kam asked.

"First we have to dig the bone out," said Dr. Brown. "That's a big job. Then we'll wrap it in wet paper. Next, we cover it with burlap strips dipped in plaster. If it's as heavy as the other bones, we'll carry it out of the park using a helicopter. Then we study it in a lab."

"In fact, Kam, I would like your class to help us dig out the bone tomorrow," Dr. Brown said. "Is your ankle well enough for you to do that?"

"Oh, yes!" Kam said. The next day, Mrs. Day's students helped to uncover the huge bone. They dug and scraped until it was time to get on the bus.

# Breaking News

When the bus pulled into the school parking lot, parents and friends were waiting. Mrs. Day had called ahead to tell about Kam's amazing find.

"Look at all the people with cameras!" Tasha said.

"There's the reporter from the newspaper who helped set up the trip," said Mrs. Day.

"Maybe we'll be on TV," said Eddie. "I'd better think of some good dinosaur jokes!"

The students stepped off the bus and into the crowd.

The reporter walked up to Kam as her parents hugged her. "So, how does it feel to be the lucky young lady who happened to find a big dinosaur bone?" the woman asked.

"It feels great!" said Kam. "I didn't think I was very lucky, but I guess I really am."

Back in school, Mrs. Day's class learned more about *Alamosaurus*. This kind of dinosaur was a plant eater. It was about 100 feet long. It weighed around 50 tons.

The students were excited when Dr. Brown e-mailed them. He said more bones from Kam's *Alamosaurus* had been found.

❋　❋　❋

One day, a few months after the trip, Mrs. Day brought a large television into the classroom. "Class, we are going to watch our friends at Big Bend National Park," she said. "They are going to lift the bone Kam found and the other bones that were found at the site."

The students gathered around the television. They watched as scientists at the dig site put ropes around a bone. Behind the scientists was a helicopter with its blades turning.

"There it goes!" a reporter said as the helicopter rose in the air. The giant bone rose, too. The students cheered.

"If you've just joined us, we're at Big Bend National Park," said the reporter. "A helicopter is removing the dinosaur bones found here last fall. It will lift each bone, one at a time, and take it several miles to where a truck is waiting. With me here is the head paleontologist on this dig. Dr. Brown, what can you tell us about this operation?"

Dr. Brown said, "Well, first of all, we owe this find to a student named Kam Ling."

Mrs. Day's students cheered again. "Hurray for Kam, the dinosaur finder!" they yelled.

"We have uncovered ten neck bones of an *Alamosaurus*," Dr. Brown went on. "Some of the bones weigh more than 1,000 pounds. The bones are being sent to the lab at the Dallas Museum of Natural History."

"Mrs. Day, do you think the bones will be shown at the museum someday?" Kam asked.

"Maybe, after the scientists have studied them," the teacher said.

"That could be our next class trip, Mrs. Day!" Eddie said. Everyone laughed.